JOJO THE KIND HEART CLOWN

ALI BAXTER

Jojo the Kind Hearted Clown

By

Ali Baxter

Contents

Jojo the Kind Hearted Clown

There was once a clown called Coco.

He was a children's show host who went on tour with his circus gang and was a great success.

However, Coco had a dark secret.

There was also a kind clown called JoJo.

JoJo was well meaning but he wasn't very good at magic tricks and often made his circus gang look bad. He'd make mistakes.

Will JoJo find out Coco's dark secret? Will he manage to solve the mystery and save the day? Or, will he make another mistake and upset the circus gang?

African Mustang Publishing

Africa - The Americas - Europe - Asia - Australasia
10 Ashley Park drive
Aberdeen
Scotland AB10 6SE

First published in Great Britain in 2022 by African Mustang Publishing

African Mustang Publishing
10 Ashley Park Drive
Aberdeen Scotland AB10 6SE

Email: vic@businessworkout.com
Tel., SMS and Watsapp: +44 790 3333 004

This book can be found at Lulu.com

Alasdair 'Ali' Baxter is a drama enthusiast turned short story writer who was born in Guildford, England and raised in Aberdeen, Scotland.

He is accomplished performer who has taken to the boards regularly as a keen member of the 'I Am What I Am', singing group, where latterly he was invited to recite Roald Dahl's "Revolting Rhymes" which included Cinderella, Little Red Riding Hood and Jack and the Beanstalk, to the delight of a number of gatherings.

Ali also participated in 'Newton Dee's Got Talent' in November 2013, his debut performance during his very first year of joining the community. To his great surprise and delight, winning first place and thereby presenting the prize two years later to his dear friend Charlie Walker.

His passion for the arts combined with his interests in films and gaming have led to this short story, where horror and theatrics collide.

Ali has future stories planned which are inspired by Roald Dahl and Stephen King, as well as a number of his favourite British sitcoms.

When he's not writing, winning competitions and enjoying a variety of sports, Ali finds time for his day job as a farmer, where he spends his time thinking up new ideas for short stories in the company of chickens and pigs.

Ali on Morevan Farm

Ali and his Acting Buddy Charlie

Productions in which Ali has performed

Peer Gynt as a Troll

Dillon Thomas as the Ice Cream Salesman

Wizard of Oz as the Tin Man

Bye Bye Birdie as Hugo Peabody
(See photo on page 23)

Princess Farmer as the Spider

Aladdin – playing the lead role as Aladdin

King Lear as the Servant
(See photo on page 24)

Joan of Ark as the English Soldier
(See photo on page 25)

Kaspar Hauser as member of a demonstration

Odysseus as Eurylochos
(See photo on page 26)

Osyris as Horace the Avenger
(See photo on page 27)

Fiddler on the Roof as Russian Soldier Fyedka

Stand Up Comedy
(See photo on page 28)

Newton Dee's Got Talent – Paint it Black
(See photo on page 29)

Performing in Toronto
(See photo on page 30)

Newton Dee's Got Talent – Buddy Holly
(See photo on page 31)

Ali at The Queen's Platinum Jubilee in 2022
(See photo on page 32)

Credits

Daisy WHITE
Running the retreat

Lisa BRACE
Mentoring
Author profile

Jonathan DANCER
Discussions

Matt BENNETT
The cover

Abi TRUELOVE
Editing the manuscript

Eric Storey
Author photos

Laura BAXTER
Encouragement
The binder

Vic BAXTER
Driver
Help with publishing

One day there was a clown called Coco. He was a children's show host who went on tour with his circus gang and was a great success. However, this clown had a dark secret. He persuaded children to become his followers and then kept them prisoners in his circus trailer, turning them into pickpockets to steal people's wristwatches and diamond necklaces while they were watching his show.

There was also a kind hearted clown called JoJo. JoJo meant well but he wasn't very good at magic tricks and often made his circus gang look bad. He made lots of mistakes. For instance he mixed up a jug that never empties with a real jug of water, and ended up pouring water over an angry man's head. He also used a real hammer instead of a rubber one to try out the unbreakable magic watch trick, and smashed a valuable gold watch from another angry member of the audience too. This made a lot of the children laugh, but the parents didn't laugh, and argued with the manager about getting a refund for JoJo's terrible performance. The manager was not pleased at all with JoJo for letting him down and told him he would be fired if he couldn't do better. The manager told him he ought to be more like Coco the Clown who was a great success with the children, and the parents thought he was a great performer too, unaware they were of his evil intentions.

One day, JoJo, desperate not to lose his job, turned for some help to his girlfriend Donna who worked as a hairdresser at a nearby salon. She said she would help him practise for his next performance, and offered to be his assistant and make sure nothing went wrong so he wouldn't get fired.

When JoJo was doing his magic trick performance, he invited Donna on stage and wanted to perform a hairdressing magic trick, pretending to cut hair when it was actually a wig.

Meanwhile, Coco felt his reputation was at stake, even though he was making more money for the circus than JoJo was. He snuck into JoJo's circus caravan with his child minions and examined the items on the dressing table.

"Okay, you know what to do, don't you!?" he ordered his minions. They all nodded nervously.

"Then do it, and don't you dare get caught or you'll be cleaning my trailer with a bucket of soapy water and toothbrushes!"

When Coco left his minions, they swapped the real scissors for toy scissors they had taken from the magic tricks box, and swapped the brown wig for a multi-coloured wig and filled the inside of it with glue, so whoever wore it would get it stuck to their head.

"We are ready for you in five minutes, JoJo!" An announcement from the ring master boomed out. JoJo dashed into his caravan and looked at his dressing table. That's funny, he thought. Where's the brown wig gone?

The audience were getting restless waiting for a show outside.

"We want a show or refund our money at once!" people could be heard shouting. The Ringmaster was trying his best to keep everyone calm.

"Don't worry folks, I'm sure it's just a few technical difficulties backstage. JoJo won't be much longer."

The Ringmaster whispered to Donna, "Where is that stupid idiot clown? Find him quickly or he is fired!"

Donna dashed backstage to find JoJo still looking for the brown wig.

"Hurry up!" Donna cried. "The audience is waiting for you!"

JoJo thought he'd found the brown wig but it was actually the multi-coloured clown wig and he grabbed it without checking it properly. He also grabbed the toy scissors, not realising they weren't the real scissors he needed.

As he passed by the Ringmaster, he grabbed him tightly by his collar and muttered crossly, "Don't you dare mess this up for your sake!" he said to JoJo threateningly. JoJo gulped hard and nodded.

The circus magic began and JoJo appeared on stage and gave a big bow to the audience.

"Welcome, you wonderful audience! Today I shall show you a hairdressing magic trick, but first I need a volunteer."

JoJo put his hand over his eyes and used his other hand to point with his finger to a member of the audience. There was a big bald man he pointed to who didn't look like he was willing to volunteer.

"You, Sir," said JoJo, "you look like a man who has a special desire to grow some hair."

The man looked astonished. "Why, I would give anything to have some hair!"

"Well," said JoJo, "This is your lucky day, because I can make hair grow on your head by magic, and my assistant Donna, who is a professional hairdresser, will assist me with this magic trick."

Donna, in the background, waved to the man grinning. The man didn't look very amused and gave a grumpy grunt in return.

"This had better be worth it!" he said crossly.

JoJo put a towel over the man's head, quickly slipping the multi-coloured clown wig (which he thought was still the brown wig) on his head first, then wiping off some glue from his hands onto his costume (how did that get there he thought) then he shouted the magic word, "Abracadabra!"

When Jojo pulled the towel away the audience gasped for a moment, and then laughed out loudly.

"What have you done!?" said the man. The multi-coloured clown wig was now glued onto the man's head. JoJo gasped in horror.

"That's not the brown wig, what happened?" he shouted to an assistant backstage. "Where is the brown wig I left on my dressing table?"

The assistant just shrugged and gave a confused expression. JoJo turned back to the man, who was now looking really mad. "Don't worry," Jojo said, trying to keep calm. "It's lucky for us my girlfriend Donna is a professional hairdresser and can fix this mix up in no time."

"Well, get on with it then!" the man said impatiently.

Donna came on stage with a portable barber's chair.

"Have a seat, sir" she said "This won't take long." The man sat in the barber's chair and JoJo handed Donna the toy scissors. She looked surprised. "These are not my scissors. Where are my real scissors?"

JoJo looked for the real scissors then shrugged, looking worried. Donna tried her hardest but the wig on the man's head wouldn't cut with the feeble attempts of the toy scissors.

"What's going on?" said the man. "Are you trying to make me look stupid?"

"No, certainly not sir, it's just some technical difficulties." said JoJo. "besides, it's just a wig, let me prove it to you." He grabbed a tight hold of the wig and pulled hard. The wig wouldn't budge. That's funny, thought JoJo, it must have got stuck tightly. He pulled even harder and the man let out a scream of pain.

"What have you done?!" the man demanded. "I thought you said it was only a wig."

"I don't understand what's gone wrong!" said Jojo. "It appears to be stuck."

"Stuck!" The man cried in horror. 'Well, you better get it unstuck and quickly too, or I am going to get you!" He grabbed a nearby crowbar that was used for building the circus tent with and raised it high.

"Now sir, please calm down, I can explain everything!"

But the man wouldn't listen and gave chase to JoJo, while swinging the crowbar wildly at him.

"THAT'S THE LAST STRAW!" yelled the Ringmaster. "YOU ARE FIRED, JOJO THE CLOWN!!"

JoJo was very upset that his circus show was a failure. He couldn't understand what had gone wrong, but he knew there was clearly some kind of sabotage involved, quite likely from his arch enemy Coco the Clown, but, since he had no proof there was nothing he could do about it.

Meanwhile, Coco now had a large number of jewels and watches he had stolen from members of the audience, by his child assistants, and he realized he had to hide them somewhere so he wouldn't get caught.

He thought for a while, and then decided to give them to the mob boss of clowns, King Loopy.

He would exchange them for lots of money and then replace JoJo to earn fame and fortune, and if he grew weary of that job, he would possibly become a hitman for King Loopy, to try and earn his trust, as King Loopy was a very tough clown that no ordinary clown dared to mess with.

On his way to King Loopy's headquarters Coco crossed paths with JoJo who was returning his magic tricks to the circus. The clowns carried identical swag bags. As they crossed paths, they bumped into each other and their swag bags went flying into the air and landed at each other's feet. "Watch where you are going, youstupid idiot!" yelled Coco. "You are an utter disgrace to clowns of all shapes and sizes!"

JoJo looked at him crossly. "I know you are somehow behind all this, and I will get you back for this one day!"

Coco laughed hard for a moment and then looked angry for being accused of what happened to Jojo's show. He hit JoJo so hard he fell backwards and landed on top of a wheelie bin, which fell over, with a heap of litter falling out of it. A stern Traffic Warden who was standing nearby heard the commotion, and hurried over.

"What's going on?" he asked, crossly inspecting the mess.

"This clown is harassing me," said Coco, trying his best to sound innocent, "and I think he might have been drinking too." he lied while trying to stifle a giggle.

"Well," said the Traffic Warden to JoJo, "unless you wish to be fined for littering you had better tidy up this mess immediately!"

JoJo very slowly and reluctantly tidied up the litter that had spilled out from the wheelie bin. The Traffic Warden turned to Coco.

"Oh you are Coco the Clown, I believe?"

"I certainly am," said Coco, brushing his clown hair back and fixing his shirt buttons to look more presentable. "Oh, I must have your autograph. My daughter loves your magic tricks and she hopes you will attend her eighth birthday which is this weekend."

"Why, I would be delighted to!" said Coco. The Traffic Warden then looked down disapprovingly at JoJo and shook his head while tutting.

"You, on the other hand, give clowns a bad name. I saw your pathetic wig magic trick you did to that poor man's head. He had to have it all shaved off in hospital and everyone laughed at him for looking so silly. If I were you, I would give up while you still can."

"Looks like he has already found a new job as a bin man. Dressed up as a clown and it suits him to a T," said Coco. The Traffic Warden laughed in agreement and high-fived Coco to congratulate him on his joke.

"Well, must I stick around and watch this loser all day, or can I get on with my duties?" asked Coco.

"Feel free to go on ahead," said the Traffic Warden. "I'll keep an eye on this litterbug and make sure he doesn't delay you any further."

"Thanks so much, sir." Coco went on his way to King Loopy's headquarters, throwing away what he thought was JoJo's swag bag into a nearby wheelie bin as he left Jojo to tidy up the litter.

"All your magic tricks are meaningless now, just like you, so I guess you won't be needing them anymore" he said to Jojo, and he then deliberately knocked over five more wheelie bins just to mock him further. JoJo flushed so red in the face with anger that even under all his makeup it was noticeable how angry he was.

"Oh dear" said Coco sarcastically, "it's a very windy day today. All the wheelie bins are blowing over. Oh well, I guess that means more work for you."

JoJo crossly picked up a half-eaten doughnut someone had thrown into the one of the wheelie bins he was currently attending to and threw it at Coco. Unfortunately, he missed and it hit the Traffic Warden's nice, clean suit instead, leaving a sticky jam stain on the yellow jacket he wore with pride while on duty.

The Traffic Warden looked suspiciously at JoJo, and then at the other wheelie bins Coco had knocked over to frame Jojo for. He took out his pencil and notebook and wrote things down while he was muttering to himself, knocking over rubbish bins, bullying famous clowns, hurling rubbish at a professional Traffic Warden and ruining his nice clean uniform.

"I would say this requires an official penalty working overtime cleaning up the streets. You are clearly a horrible delinquent of a clown as well as a nasty litterbug. I'm off to Starbucks for a brief coffee break. Supervising troublemakers like yourself is really hard work."

Coco saw the scolding JoJo was having from the Traffic Warden and set off laughing to King Loopy's, headquarters, unaware he was carrying the swag bag all this time.

When Coco arrived at King Loopy's headquarters, he was greeted by a camera which pointed towards him. A booming voice spoke out over an intercom: "WHO IS IT?"

"It's your number one clown," said Coco sheepishly. "I have plenty of loot for you my grandmaster."

The spokesman on the intercom gave a reluctant sigh, and two large double doors opened slowly.

Two strong clowns that looked like bodybuilders appeared at the bottom of a staircase. The deep voice on the intercom spoke again, "I've sent two of my assistants just to make sure you don't try to double cross me, after all, you are in debt to me, so you had better make this worth my while."

Coco gulped and started walking upstairs with the two strong clowns close behind him.

When he reached the top office, King Loopy, who was a very big, fat clown, was sitting in a swivel chair which barely contained his weight, while smoking a long cigar with his back turned to Coco.

"So, you have finally brought me some loot, have you?" he said, sounding mildly impressed.

"Yes, your royal leader, it's all in this swag bag I have brought you."

Coco handed over the swag bag. King Loopy opened it and looked inside, and then looked at Coco furiously.

"Is this a joke?" he demanded. "Do I look like I mean fun and games?"

"Oh, certainly not, your royal leader," said Coco trying hard not to laugh at the reference he made to fun and games, given he was in the presence of a clown.

"Then what do you call this!?" King Loopy emptied the swag bag with a very strong hand, all over his office desk. There weren't any jewellery and watches inside, but the circus equipment JoJo had used for his last magic show, including the toy scissors and an assortment of wigs.

"I don't understand how this could have happened," said Coco. Then he remembered running into JoJo and their identical swag bags. JoJo must be behind this thought Coco.

"It must be in the other swag bag I threw into the wheelie bin!" Coco muttered in horror.

"You threw away all the loot you stole for me!" King Loopy turned bright red in the face, looking like a volcano ready to erupt at any moment.

"Please give me some more time!" Coco begged King Loopy. "I can get it all back!"

The two strong clowns cracked their knuckles loudly at this point.

King Loopy thought for a moment, then reluctantly sighed, raising his hand to the two strong clowns to back off.

"Very well, be back here in twenty minutes or my assistants will be after you, and you will spend a very long time in a wheelchair after they break both of your legs!"

The two strong clowns nodded obediently.

Coco dashed away immediately, and was pushing every wheelie bin over in his path. The Traffic Warden saw what he was doing.

"What are you doing! Have you lost your mind?" he demanded.

"Shut up!" said Coco. "I've lost a very important swag bag and it must be found immediately!"

"Well, you'd better ask your that litterbug over there. He has been cleaning up the streets full of litter for hours now. I kept him busy in order to clean up the mess he made."

Coco ran up to JoJo and grabbed him hard by his suit collar, almost cutting off his air supply.

"Where is it?" yelled Coco.

"Where is what?" JoJo asked, trying to sound innocent.

"Don't play dumb with me; you know what I mean!" Coco yelled frantically.

JoJo thought for a moment. "If I tell you, will I get my job back as a proper clown, and you'll admit to sabotaging my magic show?"

"Yes, anything you say!" cried Coco.

"Will you stop all this child labour, return all the valuable you stole and free all those poor kids you kidnapped too?"

"YES, FOR CRYING OUT LOUD, I WILL!" Coco yelled, sounding desperate now.

"Will you pick up all this litter you have knocked over as well for me?"

"Why you little runt, I ought to choke you so hard until you pass out!" yelled Coco tightening his grip on Jojo's throat.

"Deal or no deal?" asked JoJo, while gasping for air.

"Alright. Deal." Agreed Coco reluctantly.

"In that case, it's in the rubbish truck over there that's just leaving now." Said Jojo pointing towards the rubbish truck.

"Well, why didn't you say so sooner!" cried Coco.

"Because you were choking me." said JoJo, innocently.

Coco gave an angry grunt and ran after the rubbish truck yelling, "STOP, STOP, YOU HAVE MY SWAG BAG!!"

The Traffic Warden came strolling over to JoJo.

"That was amazing," he said. "How in the world did you pull that off?"

"Oh, Coco has always been one step ahead of me since Clown College. I can literarily read him like a book," said JoJo.

"What about the swag bag? "Is it really in the rubbish truck?"

JoJo laughed hard. "Of course not," he said. "I just wanted to teach Coco a lesson. I have the real swag bag right here," JoJo turned and showed the Traffic Warden the swag bag which he had hidden under a bush.

"Wow! I must take this evidence to the police station at once. Thank you, JoJo for this stolen loot. I clear misjudged you."

So, JoJo the clown gets his job back and all the stolen goods were returned to their rightful owners.

Coco's trailer was discovered by the local authorities and the kidnapped children were reunited with their parents.

JoJo's girlfriend Donna continued to take part in his magic shows, without any further mix ups.

Coco the evil clown was tracked down and arrested for kidnapping kids and stealing priceless jewels.

However, King Loopy was not impressed by this happy ending. After watching the news in honour of JoJo making everything right again, he swore revenge upon the kind hearted clown.

He then had an awful idea.

If JoJo is the only clown who can stop us now, just imagine what we could do if he joins us? He thinks to himself.

King Loopy pushes a red button on his intercom and a droopy eyed clown called Mr Jingles enters.

"Yes, your highness," he says nervously.

"FIND OUT EVERYTHING YOU CAN ABOUT THIS JOJO THE CLOWN, AFTER ALL, I WILL NEED A REPLACEMENT NUMBER 1."

"Yes sir. Right away sir," Mr Jingles said nervously and turned to scurry away.

"Oh, before you go," said King Loopy, "You do understand the penalty for failure, don't you?"

He pushes a further button and reveals four slave clowns forced to watch a TV screen showing King Loopy telling such terrible jokes. The three clowns laugh reluctantly at the terrible jokes but one clown cried desperately to Mr Jingles, "Please, make him stop! I can't take it anymore!"

King Loopy immediately pushed another button on the intercom. "That's it, you have been warned!"

The two strong clowns arrive and promptly restrain the fourth clown tightly between themselves.

"No, no! Please! I was just joking!" the fourth clown begs, but the two strong clowns take him away all the same.

The clown screams desperately to be spared, as he is taken away by the two strong clowns, but King Loopy won't listen.

"Well he certainly won't be working in show business again!" He laughs triumphantly, then turns to Mr Jingles and shouts "Now get on with it!" orders King Loopy impatiently.

Mr Jingles nervously laughs too and runs off to finish the task while King Loopy continues laughing menacingly.

THE END

Photos from Productions in which Ali has Performed

Ali in Bye Bye Birdie as Hugo Peabody

Ali in King Lear as the Servant

Ali in Joan of Ark as the English Soldier

Ali in Odysseus as Eurylochos

Ali in Osyris as Horace the Avenger

Ali Performing Stand Up Comedy at O'Neil's in Aberdeen

Ali performing in Newton Dee's Got Talent

Ali performing at The Blues Bar in Toronto

Ali as Buddy Holly in Newton Dee's Got Talent

Ali at the Queen's Jubilee in 2022

L - #0055 - 240123 - C32 - 297/210/2 - PB - DID3479924

L - #0055 - 240123 - C32 - 297/210/2 - PB - DID3479924